EIGHTH NOTE  PUBLICATIONS

Foundations of Freedom

Carmen Gassi

Freedom is a right which should never be taken for granted. This piece is dedicated to all those who have fought to preserve the freedom of an individual or a nation. Many have fought before our time and many continue the fight today.

A lyrical middle section featuring a simple yet captivating chorale-like melody is bracketed by driving rhythms and syncopated melodies.

Carmen Gassi is a graduate of the Faculty of Music at the University of Western Ontario in London, Canada. He holds an undergraduate degree in Theory and Composition, studying composition and counterpoint with Peter Paul Koprowski, a Masters degree in performance studying clarinet with Robert Riseling and advanced conducting with Jerome Summers. Mr. Gassi has composed and arranged many works for concert band, orchestra and a variety of small ensembles. Mr. Gassi is the founding principal clarinet with Kindred Spirits Orchestra in Markham and several other orchestras and ensembles in the Toronto area.

Please contact the composer if you require any further information about this piece
or his availability for commissioning new works and appearances.

carmen.gassi@enpmusic.com

ISBN: 9781771579124   COST: $15.00   DIFFICULTY RATING: Medium
CATALOG NUMBER: BQ222551   DURATION: 4:10   Brass Quintet

www.enpmusic.com

FOUNDATIONS OF FREEDOM

Carmen Gassi

Bb Trumpet 1

FOUNDATIONS OF FREEDOM

Carmen Gassi

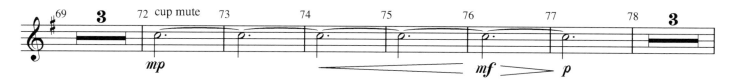

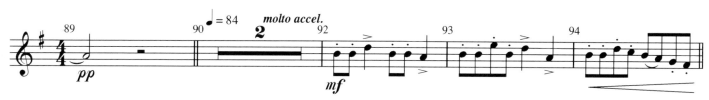

FOUNDATIONS OF FREEDOM pg. 2

B♭ Trumpet 2

FOUNDATIONS OF FREEDOM

Carmen Gassi

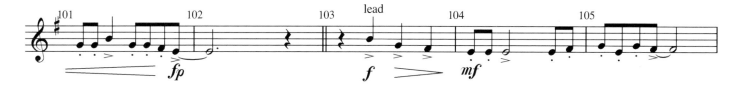

F Horn

FOUNDATIONS OF FREEDOM

Carmen Gassi

Trombone

FOUNDATIONS OF FREEDOM

Carmen Gassi

www.enpmusic.com

FOUNDATIONS OF FREEDOM pg. 2

Tuba

FOUNDATIONS OF FREEDOM

Carmen Gassi

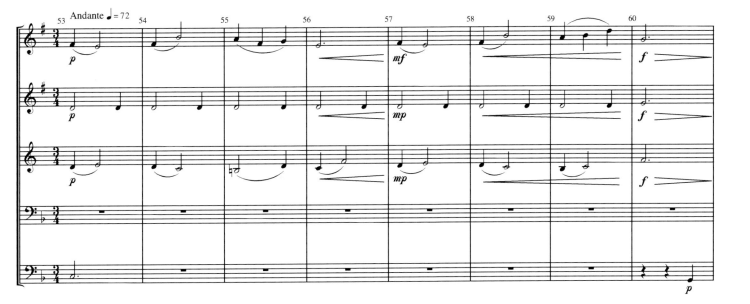

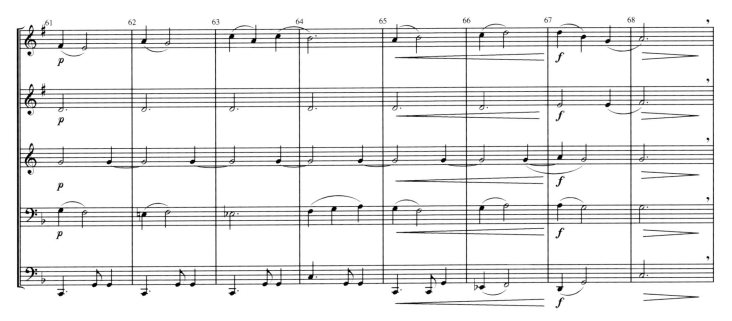

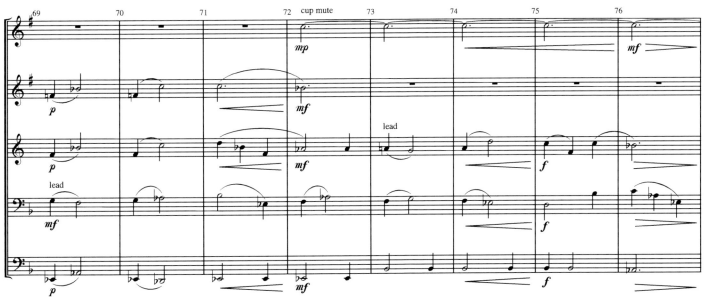

FOUNDATIONS OF FREEDOM pg. 4

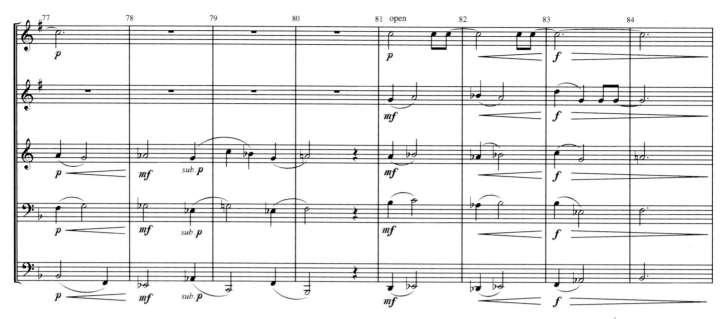